Summer 2020 —
Hell in a Handbasket

Summer 2020 —
Hell in a Handbasket

A Poetry Collection

AC Benus

an AC Benus Impression
San Francisco

Grateful acknowledgement is here offered
for the support and encouragement
I've received on the literary site
www.gayauthors.org.

ISBN 978-1-953389-01-5 (ebook)
ISBN 978-1-953389-00-8 (paperback)

SUMMER 2020 – HELL IN A HANDBASKET:
A COLLECTION OF POEMS.
Copyright © 2020 by AC Benus.

Vignette:
Marbleized endpapers from an 1849 American monograph

Library of Congress Control Number: 2020913960

Once to every person and nation
comes the moment to decide;

In the conflict of truth with falsehood,
one must stand on good or evil's side.
after James Russell Lowell

Foreword

I could not watch and be silent any longer. I know many of us have felt this way concerning the daily tumult around us. But these poems seek no apology for being raw, for raw is how most of us *have* felt. Nothing has seemed right to me for quite a long time, so this collection is also an answer for how I might 'get these out' and move on. By move on, I mean continue to reason for hope in how people come together when moments demand acts of societal bravery. It is time to wake up, both for my homeland and for the leaders of the world dealing with global emergencies, like war and the death of the Earth as habitat for mankind. It's time to wake up, or the newly coined "anthropause" will become a fixed feature.

ACB

¤{ }¤{ }¤{ }¤{ }¤
¤{ }¤{ }¤{ }¤
¤{ }¤{ }¤
¤{ }¤

Part One: Antiphrasis
From a Time of Plague I

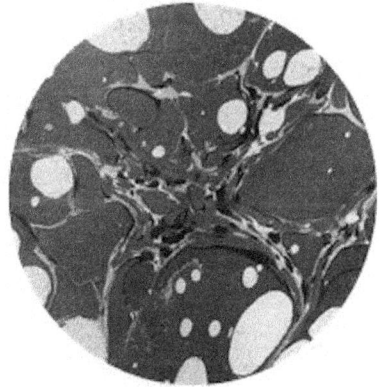

I.
Only the ignorant proudly boast
    of their ignorance.
The humble hurt to know
    they don't know everything.

The former should "Shut up the
    arrogance from their mouths."
And the latter should speak up
    more often than they do.

II.
Mortality courses through our life-blood,
For some, virus lurks there; for others, not;
As age, many feel it nipping the bud
Of a lived-life waiting to be forgot.

These times of plague fuel up the haughty man
Preaching hubris to all like-minded souls,
Blindly drawn to a death more quickly than
Powers damning simple reason's controls.

So, bleak though it may be, calm is needed,
And ears attuned to their own best accord,
Listening to those who know mortality
Courses within ourselves to be adored
By friends, spouses, and kids' vitality.

Love cannot save us, I'm afraid that's true,
But death is short when love is all we knew.

III.

The human race has rushed toward one thing,
And blithely views its own destruction still,
For the plans others pick for us are staring
dead-eyed, turning upon extinction's mill.

For now **Avarice** schemes how to abscond;
Inaction assures the worst conditions;
Billionous **Consumption**'s forced to be Donned;
Rage, **Pride**, **Rape**, **Envy** – are the new ambitions.

Fortuna turns her equalizing wheel
No more now than Justice wears her blindfold,
Because our fate's there for the Rich to steal,
While we say, act or dream nothing uncontrolled.

Seven are the traits praised today as good,
Letting Death reap virtue's final statehood.

IV.

The Four Horsemen now ride in on Hummers,
Guns blaring out a death knell randomly
Making this spring hell, like icy summers
Swamping all temperate seasons tandemly.

Seditions clothed in decades of lies come
Forward to take down what has always been hope's
Best shot for their kids to wrest from The Some
A life better outside their parent-scopes.

So, War's paved the way for wide starvation,
Winning at all Costs, Pandemic rampant,

While we of false innocent pervasion
Watch, wond'ring how things got to this extent.

Look no further than your own heart, human;
From you have the Horsemen learned their acumen.

V.

616 – the real number of the Beast

To me, at last, the answer's come
the age-old quandary now explained,
for I've understood at long last
the role granted to the dull-brained.

Seals were broken; public law smirched,
the wicked placed at the table
which world events would soon make quake
and moon-calve something horrible.

The butt-head Whore of Babylon
in his hands each a dirty bowl,
one with Iraqi oil and blood –
one, graven lucre filthy as coal.

But knowing this, what's to be done?
How to re-cage the beast that's strode
with hate these twenty years since then,
where upon War's back, new Sluts rode.
Why preach about the snively Bush
that burned with dark, Satanic fire
for profit, death, rape and sin, when
current times his goals much admire.

VI.

How right were the parents of those children
Who warned their baby-boomer brood outright
They'd ruin all with egotism bidden –
Through their congenital lack of foresight.

Now the world sees the victors of Great War,
Depression, privation, needless death wrought,
Purified by sweat and blood, are no more –
Sacrificed to the greed their bastards sought.

So how right were their folks telling them straight
The Me-Generation would bring the fall
Of all that was good, decent, in this State –
This Land's soul decimated by their gall.

Green is the callousness for Me's own kids,
Made to swim in their folks' bile-like acids. [1]

¤{ }¤{ }¤{ }¤{ }¤
¤{ }¤{ }¤{ }¤
¤{ }¤{ }¤
¤{ }¤

Part Two: Say Their Names
Black Lives Matter I

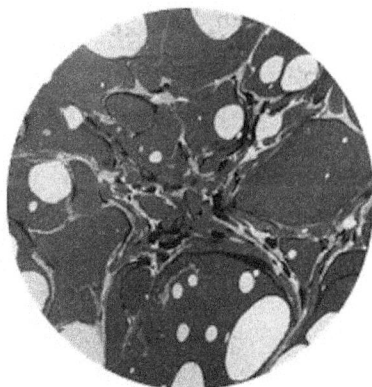

VII.

"I can't breathe"
A cry goes up
Through the Nation, while he,
Fake bone-spur coward that he is,
Hides behind the feckless brass of our generals
In the Hitler-fortress bunker beneath
The debased symbol of the White House . . .
And all because, dread reality
Wakes through the Nation –
Playtime's over.

VIII.

Secret Service with pepper spray
The So-Called dog-whistled as his
      Personal "**S.S.**"

His **S.S.** squad might deny it,
But they forget, unlike Nazis,
      Our phones capture them.

Brutal, Brutal, Brutal nightmare
The Right to Assembly gets maced
      'Fore the Peoples' House. [2]

IX.

LESSONS FOR THE KIDS

Will it never stop?

A Texas man shot cold in his
own living room by a tired
policewoman wandered into

her neighbor's apartment.
  <u>Lesson</u>: Lock your doors.
  The police might kill you.

A Kentucky woman, exhausted, as
 she's a Frontline Fighter on the
 Corona front, asleep in her bed,
 Shot eight times – asleep in her bed –
 While the cops' excuse – "Wrong apartment."
  <u>Lesson</u>: Don't fall asleep.
  The police might kill you.

A New Jersey motorist, out of
 gas on a Turnpike shoulder,
 is forced to sit in the back-of-the-
 bus seat of a State Trooper's car –
 then shot six times for daring to leave it.
  <u>Lesson</u>: Don't drive black.
  The police might kill you.

In Minnesota, a man with the
 mother of his child in the
 passenger seat, shot pointblank
 at his rolled-down car window,
 after telling the cop who pulled
 him over for no reason, that
 he had a registered revolver in
 the glovebox, and killed when
 ordered to take it out, shot point-
 blank, for no reason, with the
 man's child in the back seat.
  <u>Lesson</u>: Armed; unarmed
  The police might kill you.

Botham Jean, Breonna Taylor,
 Maurice Gordon, Philando Castile,
 there were countless more before you,

and there will be countless more
to follow your slaughters, no doubt.
> Lesson: Fuck the police.
> The police *will* kill you.

Will it ever stop!

X.

> *But the poem above*
> *Is a sham – what about*
> *All the others, you ask?*
> *What about, say . . .*

Rodney Levi – shot by RCMP in New Brunswick after a road-stop

Isiah Murrietta-Golding – 16-year-old killed, execution-style, with a single bullet to the back of his head by California police sergeant; while handcuffing the already dead boy, another cop shouted "Good shot!"

Kenneth Anthony Howard – cop-shot outside convenience store in Georgia

Olain Jefferson, Jr. – middle-aged man dragged from his hospital bed, on no charges, to die unattended in an Oklahoma jail cell

Freddie Gray – detained for no reason, then killed, handcuffed, by Maryland police in their transport wagon

Tamir Rice – 12-year-boy shot in drive-by killing by police in Ohio, playing with his red-tipped toy gun in front of his house

Michael Brown – teenager killed by police in Missouri

Eric Garner – killed by police-chokehold in New York while he begged for his life

Everett Palmer, Jr. – died with a hood over his head, his head bashed in, strapped to a chair in a New York police station after he turned himself in to clear up a past offense

Jared Lakey – 28-year-old electrocuted to death by two Oklahoma cops who tased him more than 50 times. They did not stop until the local sheriff showed up

Walter Scott – shot dead by police for a busted tail-light in South Carolina

Sandra Bland – lynched by police inside a Texas police station; her "crime"? Not putting out a cigarette fast enough in her own car when stopped for no reason

Alton Sterling – executed pointblank on the ground by a Louisiana cop

Samuel DuBose – university student killed in his car by an off duty Cincinnati campus cop

Oscar Grant III – killed on the floor of a train station by transit police in California

Hannah Fizer – 140 lbs. young woman commuting to work at 10 PM killed on the road by Missouri highway patrolman for an alleged traffic offense

Terence Crutcher – shot in the middle of a road, unarmed, in Oklahoma

Sean Bell – killed by 50 rounds of cop-bullets fired into the building from outside a club in New York

Amadou Diallo – 23-year-old unarmed sidewalk seller, cop-killed in New York

Jamar Clark – killed by police at a birthday party in Minnesota

John Crawford III – taken down by cops in an Ohio Walmart toy department

Jonathan Ferrell – shot in the back by North Carolina police on a road

Akai Gurley – cop-shot while walking downstairs at his home in New York

Meagan Hockaday – killed by California police, shot 15-inches from her face, in her own front hall

Ezell Ford – mentally ill and defenseless man put down by California cops

Ramarley Graham – killed by a cop in his own bathroom in New York

Jeremy McDole – paraplegic shot in his wheelchair by cops in Delaware

William Chapman II – unarmed 18-year-old killed by policeman in Virginia parking lot

Justine Damond – shot by a cop after she reported a rape happening behind her home

Kelly Thomas – mentally ill homeless man beaten to death by six California cops

Rayshard Brooks – shot twice in the back by a cop in a Wendy's parking lot in Georgia

Alexander Martínez Gómez – 16-year-old boy shot execution-style by a Mexican cop because he was American

Ariane Lamont McCree – killed by police while handcuffed, facedown, on a South Carolina parking lot

James Owens – seriously ill 63-year-old man shot and then tased as he lay dying in his own home by Brooklyn cops; they were there because Owens' wife had called for an ambulance

Danquirs Franklin – killed by policewoman while he was standing outside a North Carolina Burger King

Malcolm Williams – killed by an Indiana State Trooper for a broken taillight

David McAtee – killed by a Kentucky militia-man in a 7-Eleven parking lot for peacefully protesting

Tony Timpa – killed by asphyxia, begging for his life, by cops after he called 911 in Texas for medical help

Tony Green – shot in the back by a Georgia policeman on a road in the middle of the night

Daniel Shaver – killed by a cop armed with military-grade automatic machinegun; the traveling salesman, never a suspect of any crime, was on his hands and knees, crawling unarmed towards the cop, begging for his life outside his Arizona motel room

Kenneth French – developmentally challenged man killed by a cop in a California Costco; his parents there, begging for their boy's life

Javier Ambler – begged "save me" before Texas police took his life during a traffic stop

Keith Lamont Scott – killed by North Carolina police for sitting in his car, outside his own home, while his wife begged for his life; afterwards, the cops pulled down his pants and left his genitals exposed while he died slowly, alone

Korryn Gaines – unarmed woman killed in her car by Maryland police; they also shot her 5-year-old son in the backseat, leaving him alive but with permanent damage

Alfred Olango – unarmed man who called 911 for assistance with mental illness, shot multiple times by the California police who responded

Atatiana Koquice Jefferson – shot through the glass of her Texas home's back window by unannounced cop; she had been babysitting her young nephew at the time

Paul O'Neal – unarmed 18-year-old shot by two Chicago police officers in the back

Deborah Danner – 66-year-old woman shot in her own living room by New York cops

Joseph Mann – mentally ill man shot in the street by California police after the cops first tried to run him over with their patrol car

Abdirahman Abdi – killed outside his front door by cops in Ontario, who induced cardiac arrest by repeatedly punching the man's face and the back of his legs

Adama Traoré – beaten to death in a French police station for not having his ID with him

Makome M Bowole – 17-year-old boy shot in the face at close range during a French police "interrogation"

Ariel Roman – shot twice by a Chicago policewoman at a subway staircase; his 'crime'? using the unlocked doors to walk between two train cars

Laquan McDonald – 17-year-old shot sixteen times in fourteen seconds while walking away from Chicago police

Micah Xavier Johnson – suspect in a sniper shooting killed by a police bomb while sleeping in his car

Sean Monterrosa – peaceful protester kneeling on the ground, shot by a California cop five times while the 22-year-old was raising his hands in surrender

Mario Woods – shot countless times by five San Francisco policemen while he walked down 3rd Street

Luis Gongora – homeless man killed in less than 30 seconds after six San Francisco cops dragged him out of his tent; six rounds were pulled from his body

Bettie Jones – grandmother of five, killed by police bullets as she stood in the doorway of her Chicago home

Quintonio LeGrier – mentally ill 19-year-old shot seven times in the same Chicago incident that killed Bettie Jones, who was trying to save his life

George Floyd – killed by asphyxia, begging for his life, in Minnesota

Ahmaud Arbery – jogger shot three times with a shotgun at close range by three men 'deputized' by local police in Georgia; before being shot, he was hit from

behind by one of the men's pickup trucks; then the
killer spat out *"F_____ N_____!"*as Arbery lie dying
in the middle of the road

*And these victims merely
scratch the surface,
and most only happened
in the last five years.*

*So, what about them,
dear reader?*

*Can we really believe
anyone claiming
not to "get" the
BLM movement
anymore...?*

*If they try, don't believe them
Or their lie for a second; they know.
They know this is the way they like it.*

*So don't believe anyone
who says they don't understand
the issues – because after all –*

*You owe it to the people
named here, and the
many, many, many
more not named here,
not to believe their lies.* [3]

XI.

Protest.
One foreign headline said it all:
"Peaceful Protests Against
Police Brutality Met With Shocking Wave
Of Police Brutality."

Protest.
The fake 'Open the Economy Now'
Stars and Bars tanktop-wearing goons
Praised for the "bravery" of making sure
Covid burns like fever through the Black Economy.

> Do you care? One headline
> Mean more to you than the other? [4]

XII.

Words are my curses and blessings.
They hurt their creator – me – more
To set down methodically, one by one,
Than for an aghast reader
To breeze through them.

> Curse and blessing.
> It can be no other way.

XIII.

OLE HATRED'S SONG

Refrain:
Rand Paul, so-called Kentucky 'Senator',
but really just another get-rich-quick bigot,
deserves the wrong-side of History footnote
he's made of himself. Yes, sir!

Chorus 1:
When asked about his opposition to Gay Rights
    protections from being fired from a job
    for one's orientation, he said with a tut-tut:
    "Well, they shouldn't be doing
    that at work."

(recap Refrain: *Rand Paul . . . just . . . another bigot,* etc.)

Chorus 2:
When actively opposing making lynching
    a Federal hate crime, he said: "Not needed!"
    Such measures of White Justice are things
    of the good-ole past . . . . Meanwhile, two in
    California, so far, have been found hanging
    from trees before Old Glory flag poles.

(recap Refrain: *Rand Paul . . . rich-quick . . . footnote,* etc.)

Chorus 3:
When pressed to show his true colors of
    hatred for all 'not his kind,' we learn he
    thinks LGBT+ folks are no better than
    the dirty-word "homo . . . *SEX*-ual" means
    in his wide-stance, toe-tapping
    grease trap of a brain.

We learn his defense of lynching
    caused others of his same "Birth
    of a Nation" criminality to display
    Black men – like Christ on a burning cross –
    hanged from a tree, as blood
    sacrifice to the Stars and Stripes;
    to the Powers that Be.

Refrain:
Rand Paul, so-called Kentucky 'Senator',
but really just another get-rich-quick bigot,
deserves the wrong-side of History footnote
he's made of himself. Yes'ems, boss!

And *they* wonder why we kneel
at the National Anthem;
And they wonder why the flag
is burned at protests. [5]

XIV.

. . . so many dead . . .
and for what . . .

All 'guilty' of having their lives
encounter that of a cop's
who'll go home to dinner
after a hard day of killin'!

All 'guilty' of living in a land where
police are permitted to be
the alpha-omega of anyone's life –
their Judge, Jury and Executioner.

. . . but will they really let
things be changed . . . .

¤{ }¤{ }¤{ }¤{ }¤
¤{ }¤{ }¤{ }¤
¤{ }¤{ }¤
¤{ }¤

Part Three: House of Mirrors

But Where Will We Live . . . I

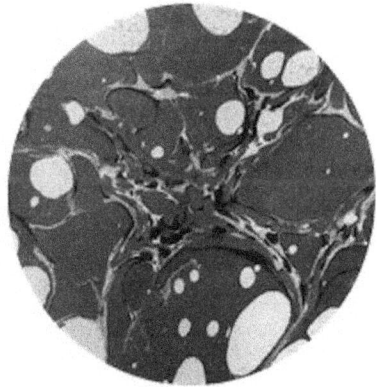

XV.

How long the day of reckoning
    Has hounded our every footfall,
While we thought the shopping easy –
    And the chosen choices could stall
Payment on a bill whose interest
    Would cost our kids their very all –

We went on indulging the same,
    Like Times had not caused our repine,
Forked tongues saying greed was harmless,
    But minds knowing the check-out time
To give Nature's owed pound of flesh
    Fast approached to pay for our crime.

So now, with the world on fire
    From Siberia to Brazil;
From Patagonia to Perth;
    With Dust-Bowl dryness on our sill,
We walk and complain of the heat
    Knowing the worst's yet to come still. [6]

XVI.

An enraged Earth plays flame-tag with itself,
Saying in thunder and tossed-aside embers
From asshole humans and their lit cigarettes,
"You shall burn for this! You shall die fittingly."

And so, fire touched upon the tinder dry,
Storms and licks and leaps over quickening winds

To decimate first the Northern Hemisphere
All through its long half-year furnace summers.

And then, this fire touched in tinder dry
Storms and licks and leaps without a pausing rest
To decimate too the Southern Hemisphere
All through its long half-year oven summers.

Temperance gone, the North Star sheds a tear in smoke,
But it's only the orange tinge of pollution
We tell each other is "charming" at sunsets,
Knowing the brown coal-smog signals Man's sunset.

The Southern Cross appears to drip tears of blood
From the starry crown of satellites one man's
Allowed to link, like a fishing net of death,
To rob the dying even of a clear sky.

Therefore, an Earth enraged shuttles the planchette
Above continents, like a cruel boy using
A magnifying glass to set ants on fire –
Only the "ants" are preserves, fields and forests.

She spells out a mighty Ouija damnation,
For it will all go: Yosemite and Muir Woods;
The remnant margins of the Once-Amazon;
The well-raped and cleared teak lands of Borneo;

Siberia; Canada; Japan; China;
The Middle East; Australia; Europe; Belize;
South Asia; North America; Germany;
And every other refuge for Man will go.

The world's empirically on fire, while we fiddle.
Time's up. We've had our chance, now Nature demands

Our pieces be removed from this world's chessboard,
Laughing flames when we cry, "But . . . where will we live . . . !"

XVII.

Damn our constant thirst for "Good News!"
 If it's good news you want
How about giant viruses
 Revived from permafrost –
Each Pleistocene-sized and dormant
 Thirty-five thousand years –
But now global warming melts them
 And they spring back to life.

  There's some of your "Good News!"

Then there's the Pacific Northwest
 Where another headline,
For June-2020 readers,
 Proclaims micro-plastic
Burned up as Asian pollution
 Rains down now by the tons
To smother the Cascade Forests
 To the point of their death.

  There's some of your "Good News!"

Don't forget the Dump-heads changing
 Sovereign Alaskan law
So Donny Dump Junior can shoot
 All the bear cubs he wants –
OR, the Conservation Officer
 Fired in Canada

For refusing to shoot bear cubs
    Whose mother he'd already killed.

    Had enough of your "Good News" [7]

XVIII.

HYMN

Global Warming, God's gift to Man –
    Now one hundred thirty-five-degree days
    Can force a mad migration to The North,
    As a billion Indians try to breathe.

    Now a hundred fifty-degree days
    Can roast the poor out of the Gulf States,
    While the Rich's AC adds to the sweat.

Global Warming, Man's gift to God –
    Now locust swarms, vaster than fields of rice,
    Can return Biblical Times to people
    And fill up the opium-parlor churches.

    Down on your knees, you hopeless feckless God;
    The Dollar, Greed and Death are the truest
    Trinity since we've gone over the brink.

Global Warming, just some Fake News –
    Death and Destruction's Art has fooled us all,
    At least as it's advertised in public,
    Despite what is known in our heart of hearts.

It's more comfortable to believe a lie
Totally unworthy of any faith,
Save the one that says "You must keep what's yours." [8]

    Amen.

Part Four: The Maggot
From a Time of Plague II

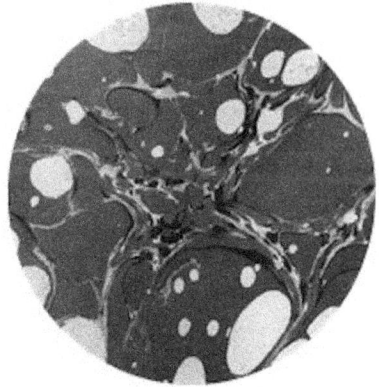

XIX.

From this point in time when Death stalks the land,
A brandy-burning from the throat pray tells
Future generations to take their stand
And not drink the koolaid of poisoned wells.

Each tragedy is individual,
As involute, we must each go alone
On to the Dark where we'll answer in full
For the loam of guilt couching our tombstone.

So learn no lie political can live
In the purifying air of death:
There'll come a time when every truth will give
Testimony to what we did with breath.

Burns the killed-throat with the brightest knowing;
The forthright liquor of Truth brooks no forgoing.

XX.

Like a length of hose with a million holes,
The stub of a So-Called man super soaks
His dope-addled groupies of the false polls,
To flood the Supremacist wet-dream of folks.

Therefore, think you actions of the courts, or
The cops' brutal license to murder all,
Is unrelated to Gop plans for the poor
Where fear, prison, silence governs wherewithal.

For no, there's no accident now at work
But collusion from The Blue and The Red,

And the gown-wearing Judges who can smirk,
Doling out injustice, and not bread instead.

No healthcare; no caring; no Liberty –
For those the Rich brew the bitterest tea.

XXI.

Modern politics
    like modern police

Pull the gun out first
    then gin themselves up

A fake 'How it Happened'
    excuse for the crime.

Yes, the mayhem wrought
    'Got the fucker!" style

From behind the public's
    blank check, who-cares, shield.

XXII.

Like stigmata, are we never to see
The wounds of others inflicted on us?—
Yet have the willful arrogance to be
Those with "I'm saved!" crusted on lips like puss –
Content to let others bleed for our sins?
What happened to true Christian thoughts of shame? –
That we don't do enough when life begins
To let inequity assume the blame
For our guilty choice of complicity.

How we've turned our backs on the way of Christ,
And do it shamefully in Greed's interest,
Graven 'salvation' set where vacancy
Excised neurotic souls sold for and priced
At what thirty silver coins value best.

XXIII.

The So-Called's Juneteenth Tulsa Debacle;
June 20, 2020

*Ninety-nine years and one day after
the Nation's deadliest mass lynching
and firebombing of African Americans*

Dog-whistle politics eat their brains,
And though to you and me – and people good –
The Torch-Light Rallies of the Dotard's strains
Of hissing nonsense can't be understood,
To the Fascist-of-Heart the doubletalk
Speaks a necrotic language of action.
White hood clad, machinegun-toting black-hawks
Hear Putin's Puppet with no distraction.
"A November election lost," he says,
Snickering with raw meat for his bitches,
"You'll know what needs to be done to that 'prez'"—
Nothing less than civil war he pitches.
    As he's a bald-faced enemy to The Constitution,
    Trump's a maggot in the American Institution. [9]

XXIV.

In the ign'rant psychosis of the times,
The excess in Trump's subtext of blame shows
He charges others for his exact crimes,
Dreading their innocence while his guilt grows.

Clinton was 'crooked,' while Joe is 'withdrawn';
Obama equals treason – the Don knows
Is bullshit – 'cause he's traitor and Russian pawn,
Trembling at the rope's end of a new repose.
    So, the seventy-four-year-old coward
    Practically begs for trial and conviction,
    His soul's last chance to atone for what's soured
    A more Perfect Union through malediction.
        At last free then from under Putin's heel,
        He'll make of his final sounds something real. [10]

¤{ }¤{ }¤{ }¤{ }¤
¤{ }¤{ }¤{ }¤
¤{ }¤{ }¤
¤{ }¤

Part Five: Depraved Heart

Black Lives Matter II

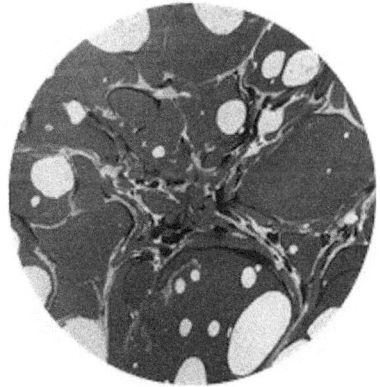

XXV.

Farewell to thee,
June, 2020, fictional lives –
   No more will we see
      Grinning Darkie Toothpaste man,
      Or our dear help,
      Those live-in caricatures
      Of make-believe 'Good Ones'.

      No more will we buy
      Aunt Jemima pancake mix,
      Or steam Uncle Ben's broken rice;
      Goodbye to Cream of Wheat's
      Smiling 'boy' of a train cook.

Farewell to thee,
June, 2020, actual lies? –
   No more will we see
      Jimmy Fallon in blackface?
      Or what about
      Jimmy Kimmel in shoe polish?
      We're sure their types are gone . . . ?

What about us,
June, 2020, maligned Gay lives –
   No farewell we see
      To "In Living Color" screams
      Stereotypes;
      Caricatures of limp-wrist
      "Modern Family."

      No farewell we see
      To "South Park" anger-filled hatred

Stereotypes;
Trans mockery, Big Gay Al,
'F__' hurled every episode.

Farewell to thee,
June, 2020, actual bigotry? –
    No more blackface seen
        But Gay youth taught self-loathing
        Through pop media
        Gets no mention or protest,
        Except for my voice, here.

XXVI.

A picture book of history
Can be made of more than pictures;
It can be the sights, sounds and smells
Captured in words at the moment.

My high school history book had
A snap of a white thug ramming
A Black person with a flagpole
Named "The Soiling of Old Glory."

The *moments* happening now have
Cops spitting out on Blacks they've just killed:
"Looks like a closed casket, homie,"
And then laugh and laugh on video.

Future books will have that 'moment'
As well as Officer Rolfe kicking
Rayshard Brooks dying on the ground,
Then boasting on tape: "I got him."

Another pic our kids should see:
Minnesota's criminal charge

Against the cop who kneeled 9 minutes,
Painfully taking George Floyd's life,
Acted out of a "Depraved Heart"
And disregard for human life –
But will the books capture
How the cop was trained that way?

People are wrong who say history
Is written through statues and stones;
History's formed through blood and tears,
And always via sounds and sights.

XXVII.

"I'd do it all over again,"
Boasted Garrett Rolfe,
    Saying a week after the fact, that
        1) He has the privilege to kill
           whomever he wants, and
        2) Black lives don't matter to
           his depraved heart.

This is the heart of the matter
Every goon means when he dares
    Shout "Blue Lines" mean more than
        1) every minority victim ever deprived of
          their existence by the whim of a cop, and
        2) Black lives will never matter to
          cops' depraved hearts.

      Boasting in one voice,
      "We'd do it all over again!"

XXVIII.

Minstrel Faces, 2020

The BLM Movement I've seen,

In the last few months of crucible heat,
Culturally appropriate
Elements of our hard Gay Rights struggles
Without any thought at all.
They've taken ACT UP's protest wakeup call
Of how Silence = Death,
Twisted round to silence equals violence;
This Stepin Fetchit moment
Of usurping the Larry Kramer ode
To straights' passive allowing of
Extermination of Gays by disease
For their active killing by cops.
So too BLM's appropriation,
In paint and chalk stenciling
Of "Black Lives Matter" in rainbow colors.
Taking from us our symbols,
Each soaked in the blood of Gay patriots,
With no consideration;
With no acknowledgement of their background.
It's BLM's own form of
Privileged elitism: The assumption –
Without asking – that Queer folks
Will stand with them, by standing up for them,
While African Americans
In the broader Equality Movement
These long decades have stood next
To ugly white oppression, coming to
A hateful Mammy-ism
On 'How gays are' – lisp-cowards, sick, twisted,
Deserving of all the privations of legal
Protections that their labeled
Projections of a "lifestyle choice" deserve.
Thanks, BLM, for getting
Gay cops and their fams banned from Pride marches –
Which is not ancient history –
But your campaign of three years;
I guess you're too blind to see
How other minorities suffer in
The world's policing units

To advance Blacks and every oppressed group.
  So where's that apology
For all your gross bigotry of the past?
  No intentions of amends???
Well, don't worry – we never thought you would.
  But yeah, we *will* stand by your side
Because we know it's the right thing to do.
  So, how about you showing
You actually have our backs as well?
  Hmm? Speak up; I can't hear you . . . . [11]

XXIX.

DEFINITION

Depraved Heart /di-**prayv**-dt·harr-**t**/
PROPER NOUN (pl. Depraved Hearts) the social affliction of
malice aforethought felonies, most closely associated
with police criminality; synonymous with **Shoot to Kill**.

Example: "The police union attempted to deny
Depraved Heart 101 is taught at police academies,
despite the widespread display of police shooting to kill
defenseless members of the public."

— ORIGIN Latin *depravis cori, aperta urna puer-
domum* (or, "looks like a closed casket, homie.") [12]

XXX.
What happens to a soul
Made to seethe in frustration –
Made to boil in the bile
Of how man treats man?

At Fahrenheit 173, wine on a burner
Gives up its invisible vapor of alcohol;
At that temperature, does the wine of a soul
Let go of its anger, or of its immortality?

Can a spirit boiled
In the hatred of others
Long survive in a world
That can't be bothered to give a damn?

XXXI.

"Now"

All in good fun – what bullshit.

Consider this – black stereotypes
Were forced off the air and out of movies
In the 1950s – sixty fucking years ago.
Asian Chickenman, Ms. Swan insults
Forced off the air in the 1990s – thirty fucking years ago.
So when will LGBT caricatures be killed?
SNL's Jimmy Fallon Scrooge as a flaming f____t sketch;
(Why should he not have to apologize for this offensive
Portrayal of Queer people, if he's forced to do it for a
Blackface sketch? Where's the justice? Anyone . . .?)
What about Fred Armisen's continual portrayal of Gay people

As nothing but H-word sex fiends; self-loathing
Is at the root of his puerile, thumb-sucking hate, no doubt.
(This so-called man really should seek help for his anti-gay ingraining,
And be barred from peddling it anymore in public.)
Or the infuriating Modern Family episode where
Members of the LGBT Community are made to think a
Fifty-year-old man and ten-year-old boy are "getting gay
Married," and the decent-minded public just
Has to accept it.
So, I repeat, when will we – as the LGBTQ+ Minority –
Stop letting our kids be debased by straight-hate
If it is not NOW?!
All in good fun – my ass. [13]

XXXII.

And...what about equal justice

When these murdering cops
    Were arrested – Oh, such a
    Recent trend –

Were they thrown to the ground,
    Faces shredded against asphalt,
    Shackled bleeding with knees pinning
    Their backs and throats?

No? So, you murdering cops weren't treated
    Equally to the way you treated those
    Moments before they died?

Now, how about some *equal* justice;
    What ya say, boys in blue?
    If the humiliation you dispensed
    So liberally on others was good enough
    For them, it's good enough for you –
        And you know it.

AH . . . that's why you're scared;
    Now I get it, you 'Blue Lines Matter'
    Pants-shitters. [14]

¤{ }¤{ }¤{ }¤{ }¤
¤{ }¤{ }¤{ }¤
¤{ }¤{ }¤
¤{ }¤

Part Six: Curtains of Dust

But Where Will We Live . . . II

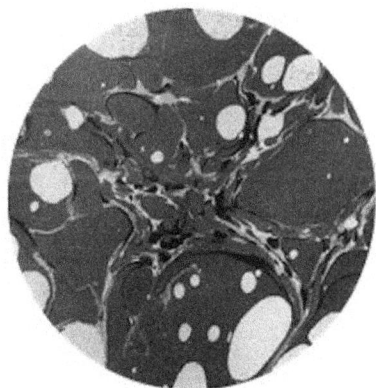

XXXIII.

From east to west come desert sand,
    For wild weather's the norm new
Driving out all mild temperance
    While wishing this were a snafu.

Situation normal's all fucked up,
    Replaced with Saharan sand storms
Choking Florida and Georgia,
    Burning throats and eyes in swarms . . .

        It's just what COVID-19 folks,
        What with their respiratory health
        More precarious than ever, need;
        To have aerosolized sandpaper
        To rasp and grate and shred their lungs
        In times as turbulent as these.
        I have lived through such dire attacks,
        For above Tokyo one fine year,
        Toxic clouds of silica blew,
        Raised from the dunes of the Gobi.
        Awful, searing burn in the nose
        Settled down-throat into the lungs,
        Inviting respiration to
        Feel like gargling with glass.
        I wheezed and wheezed for weeks after,
        And now the American South
        Feels Gobi's African cousin.
        But still people will vote for the
        "Global Warming is Fake News!" Gops?
        Lord help their kids, who'll have to bear
        The brunt of their parents' evil
        'The future does not matter' selfishness.

Situation normal's all fucked up,
    Replaced with Saharan sand storms
Choking Florida and Georgia,
    Burning throats and eyes in swarms.

From east to west come desert sand,
    For wild weather's the norm new
Driving out all mild temperance
    While wishing this were a snafu . . . . [15]

XXXIV.

And we thought the Scopes Monkey trial
    Pitted reason against foolishness –
Science against crackpot 'belief' –
    When we learned all about it in school.

So how could we have de-evolved
    From a country of progress and hope –
From a nation laughing at morons –
    To inbred, 'Deliverance' zealots?

Simple – Pat Robinson's whisper
    Into Nixon's too-distracted ear
Led to shameless Gop pandering;
    Just to get the degenerate-vote.

Decades later, and here we are:
    Faith's a placebo, the fourth monkey
In a blue-suit, red-tie wearing
    Line of those who refuse to do good.

The 'see no good'; the 'hear no good';
    The 'never speak' a wholesome word perverts –
Genetically depraved mutants –
    Hell-bound for the evil they have done.

For the last-to-follow monkey,
    The fourth Franken-Simian's the worst;
He sits on a glut of self-praise
    As guardian idol to 'DO no good'.

So now we ask how we de-evolved
    From a country of progress and hope –
From a nation laughing at morons –
    To inbred, 'Deliverance' zealots?

And we thought the Scopes Monkey trial
    Pitted reason against foolishness –
Science against crackpot 'belief' –
    When we learned all about it in school.

XXXV.

Science swelters under the heat lamp of
            avoidance
            willful disbelief's
            selfish disregard

It leaves the rest of us parched to the bone
            broiled in ignorance
            de-fleshed by politics'
            selfish disregard

XXXVI.

    These days and weeks go by alone
And I feel I can't get any fresh air;
    The freeway noise never lessens
As I know I can't get any fresh air.

Perhaps the virus is in me
At the level of each cell strangling
   Oxygenation's needed path
As the lifeforce of each cell is strug'ling.

   Worse yet, I can't afford water
That costs **100%** more these days
   Than a few mere years in the past;
Which costs **100%** more these days.

   Baby-boomers refused to tax
Themselves to pay for the system's upkeep,
   Preferring offshore tax shelters
While our American cities crumbled.

   And so, I thirst; can't get enough
Water to save the cell structures I need;
   From Covid and Conservatives,
There's no water to save the structures we need. [16]

XXXVII.

And to think—
   The proverbial glass of water used to be
   Free in this country, while now, working
   Men and women this June can't even afford
To buy what's on tap.

XXXVIII.

It seems the Powers-that-Be proliferated
All the poisoned waters now contaminated
From Flint, Michigan, to Russian arctic oil spill –
Every drop once fit to drink, now dosed to kill.

Evidence the benzine flames from deep-shale fracking
North American tap water is not lacking;
Or massive dams designed to drown all trace of life
On continents where Water Wars erupt in strife.
We can only cover parched mouth and nose and ask,
Strug'ling against the grown discomfort of our mask,
Who from behind this curtain of dust pulls the strings
That famine, pandemic and blood-red chaos brings?
Yet, we know the answer before our hand can draw
The screen aside to expose who breaks Nature's law –
Those out to make money; those few who *will* profit
And damn our eco-souls to the very last bit. [17]

XXXIX.

The toxicology of H_2O,
The spray poisons on crops,
The DDT on human flesh . . .

Is it any wonder Pollyanna journalistic
Practices swept under the rug the inconveniently
(Boring) fact of a worldwide insect collapse?

A theme they thought a joke – "What's a few
Bugs, anyway? Ha-Ha" – and one that wouldn't
Sell ad space is fine to ignore; but now, it's
        coming home, too late.

Only this year have news outlets reported the
scientific fact – 50% of Earth's bug biodiversity
is gone, already. Gone. Dead. Never to recover;
        an event larger than any dino die-off.

Anyone who can look at that and think "So
What," I'll tell you, you are part of the problem.
The food Domino Effect is well underway, whether
        you care or not.

Half insect populations mean, lizard, reptile,
Fish, birds dying in droves; the things that eat
them as well, and up and up until the
            only 'meat'

You and I will have to eat will be human.
Is that headline so funny? Is that prospect
A "So what?" for your kids and grandkids? [18]

XL.
Anger, Anger, Anger –
      our world's lost,
            set afloat
                  on a river
                        of Anger.

XLI.
Many years ago
I headed a poem
"I sigh and wonder why."

Today, near the threshold
Of a July that seems doomed,
Even before its first sunrise,

"I sigh and wonder why"
For a different reason:
One of Tipping Points and inaction.

      I had to look it up, for I could hardly believe it:
      Al Gore's movie declaring a climate emergency
      Came out in 2006; or, some 14 years ago.
      And what has happened in all that time we've allowed to pass?
      Faith-based ecology grounded on belief-based 'science,'

For so far over the rational tipping point we have gone,
That not even empiric measure can escape the mire
Privately-funded politics have quick-san'd the human race.
In our hubris, we've forced the Earth herself to find an answer –
And though she cries pointed tears about it, her one weapon
Is poised above every human neck in the here and now –
A major extinction is her only way to survive
And she will do something before it's too late, unlike us,
And she'll draw a little comfort to know we're sent to sleep
Dull and doped by the narcotic of our 'faith' and 'belief.' [19]

¤{ }¤{ }¤{ }¤{ }¤
¤{ }¤{ }¤{ }¤
¤{ }¤{ }¤
¤{ }¤

Part Seven: A Less Perfect Union

From a Time of Plague III

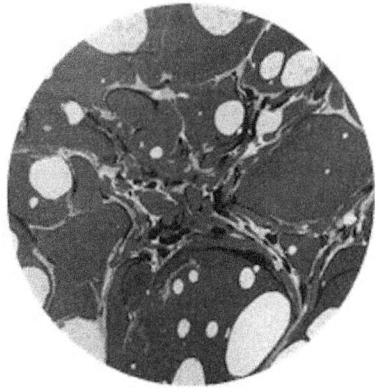

XLII.

Those Sitting on Thorns

Profound of harm is Cyber's deep Spy State,
Network-casting an indiscriminate
Phishing sweep o'er those who can't concentrate,
And thus, know not what fate is imminent.

Each of us is made criminal when they
Are allowed to police down our ideas
Entrapped illicitly, yet made parley
Felony charges as panaceas.

They watch our every move online, and wait
Till we can be censored with their baton,
For now they've passed so many laws, we're all
Dollar signs to the Private Police State
Leeching public funds for its magic wand
To pay for "law & order's" crystal ball. [20]

XLIII.

"After this I witnessed another angel
Descending from the heavens on high.
So glorious appeared his authority,
The entire Earth became enlightened
When the command of his voice
Sang out its woe:

'Fallen, fallen is the Nation Once Great!
She's become but a crash-house for fiends.
She's but safe harbor for the greedy and uncaring soul;
A refuge for every jackdaw, dripping with carrion gore.

For she has forced all Peoples drink
    The toxic liquor distilled from
The profanity of material lust.
    The leaders of the Earth have been coerced
To engage in venereal commercial
    Intercourse with her,
And the Wall-Street elite of the world
    Screw her to sink in more depravity luxurious
        From her lack of moral integrity.'"
                    —Book of Revelations 14:6-8

XLIV.

Stupidity swings the loudest sledgehammer
Mobs far drunk on Destruction's lust might employ
To uproot masonry's work, while they clamor
Slogans that don't consider what they destroy.
For they'd condemn two Presidents' lives in bronze
Who jointly worked a pure, single sheet of gold
Ensuring that Good *could* break slavery bonds
And spell out no one's soul can be bought and sold.
Assassinate Lincoln then a second time;
Throw ropes round Grant's and his neck in ignorance
That Abe gave his life to pay for the South's crime
And write 'Black Lives Matter' in drops his blood imprints.
    So pause your Movement in your passion's fire;
    Build, don't wreck monuments there to inspire!

XLV.

June Rollcall at the Supreme Court

Is there a right lyrical form
    To sing of a court that avows

'Equal Justice Under the Law'
    And hints at what those words espouse?
For Rights, five justices made clear
    Party loyalty is a crime
If it asks to deprive freedom
    At this dangerous point in time.

    For, see how the Gops reacted?—
    Immigrant kids allowed to stay;
    Equal rights for Gays, at long last;
    A woman's control over her
    Reproductive health reinforced.
    For the Dreamers specifically,
    These innocent kids of migrants,
    The Republican Admin acts
    As dumb as water-boards,
    Saying the law passed by Congress,
    Affirmed by courts, top to bottom,
    Is still "unconstitutional."
    They either slept through their high school
    Civics 101 classes, OR
    Have no idea how our nation's
    Establishment makes it all work . . . .
    OR . . . or, this Administration
    Is the one unconstitutional
    Enemy of The People here.

Knowing this explains the brown pants
    Republicans are seen wearing
As they go 'bout their daily lies
    With a Court their shit now airing.

Next on the justices' docket?
    Demanding Trump show his Russian ties –
Putin's thrall must show his taxes
    And with it, the Gop party dies. [21]

XLVI.

After three-plus years
    There's a bitter taste lingering
In the former phrase
    Of a "more perfect union."
From sore Gop misuse
    It's sat festering shallow,
Like some bad strep throat
    After laying neglected –
Stagnant water stuck
    As if in a plumbing trap –
Bitter on the tongue
    Barfed up from Republican
Gullets of disease.

XLVII.

This election year, I stumbled upon
The first candidate speeches recorded
More than a hundred years dead and long gone
Off'ring us what 1912 afforded.
Wilson, Taft and Roosevelt each had goals
That make today's Progressives seem backward;
And Gops, cowardly extremists, sold-souls.
We've lost so much since those speeches were heard.
    In less than thirty, the Gops have taken
    Values back a hundred and fifty years –
    Poof – progress gone in the vapor of hate.
    They've convinced forward movement's mistaken,
    Replaced with poverty, too many tears
    And internal conflicts that now seal our fate. [22]

XLVIII.

Divide & Conquer

It's the only way bad guys can win,
But just pause a moment and think
   What if things had gone right?

        – No Ronnie Recessional;
        No King Bush the First.

        – No King Bush the First;
        No blubbering Butt-Head Criminal
        Slut-Brained The Second.

        – No blubbering Butt-Head Criminal
        Slut-Brained The Second;
        No Dumpster-Diving in a nation
        Starved for social, immigration,
        Economic, medical, racial, LGBT – etc., etc.,
        etc. – justice and leadership right now.

        – And because of Trump,
        No new president ever again?

   But, what if things had gone the right way?
Just pause a moment and think before you vote
Because Divide-n-Conquer is the *ONLY* way they can win. [23]

XLIX.

The Heavy Toll of "Leadership"

<u>Ron</u>:
"Clean up Berkeley," 1966, "a haven for communist sympathizers, protestors, and *sex* deviants [meaning F__s]."

<u>Toll</u>: 1 dead, 1 blinded, 32 in intensive care after police open fire with assault rifles on college students.

<u>Dick</u>:
"Listen, the boys on college campuses today," 1970, "are the luckiest people in the world."

<u>Toll</u>: Ohio militia guns down 9 victims, and sends another to the morgue. Mississippi cops beat 14 college kids; 2 fatally.

<u>Don</u>:
"They're my people," 2017.

<u>Toll</u>: Charlottesville hate-riot. Local police stone and mace peaceful counter-protestors, letting Neo-Nazis mow them down with cars – killing at least 1 and sending 10 more to the ER. In the Summer of 2020, this has become Trump's "My People's" way of terrorizing anti-hate demonstrators. [24]

L.
What if; what if

Advancement had not evaporated
In the vapors of their hate.

What if

> Hate-mongers hadn't weaponized fear
> To assault the very notion of progress?

LI.

Malachi might warn of Nature's viral fire
  Refining mankind; making the high, low:
Exalting through valleys like a death-fed pyre –
  Declaiming no difference in ashes though.
Consider COVID the Environment's rage –
  A social distancing before the curtain
Falls on our brief moment upon the Earth' stage
  And we're heckled to the sidelines for our sin.
Cowled Death waits in the wings for us with its
  Once benevolent sweep of a shepherd's crook
That keeps us away from harm while it still permits
  A taste of the freedom from all it might brook.
    But now that gentle curve is iron scythe
    To mow down and extinguish human life.

LII.

Division, mayhem,
Un-American behavior and morals
Total debasement
Of optimistic morale, started with
Amoral toad, Gingrich.
So it's nat'ral Gop politicizing
Of 'entitled' rage
Rots the flesh of American Decency
Like frostbitten hearts
Locked in the chest of Repub depravity.

LIII.

This summer, Death unchecked across the land,
Political vendetta makes The Trump
Now of all times insist the Supreme Court dump
The Rights to insurance already in hand.
What's Donnie's obsession to countermand
Obama's laws like a dog in mid-hump,
Mad in his mind, foaming, doddering grump,
Who doesn't care he's Custer at his last Stand.
    Real people with real jobs are dying out there,
    When the affordable health act is all they have
    To save their children's lives with Obamacare,
    And this cheese-puff dictator, cracked pot of salve
        Demand this last bastion of decency "fall"
        To slay a higher percentage of us all. [25]

¤{ }¤{ }¤{ }¤{ }¤
¤{ }¤{ }¤{ }¤
¤{ }¤{ }¤
¤{ }¤

Part Eight: "Slaughter Them F...... N......!"
Black Lives Matter III

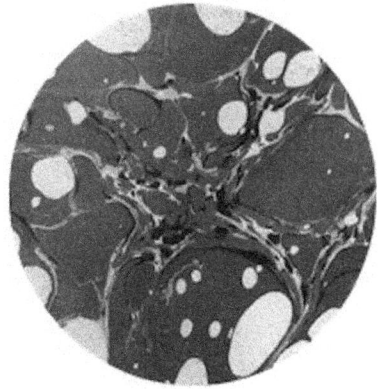

LIV.

. . . Meanwhile, back in Louisville . . .

No charges brought yet –
Justice turns a blind eye to them –

    The thugs with badges
        Who stole the life of a sleeping
    Breonna Taylor,
        Like marauding thieves in the night,
    Have lived the high life.
        When they breathe, they flaunt their freedom,
    Knowing just like crooks,
        They've gotten away with murder.

    They think it's their right
        To use "wrong address" as pardon –
    Malice afterthought –
        To keep their jobs and liberty;

To never question
    their job security means more
than all their killed victims'
    corpses piled at the police doors.

    Do you want the proof?—
        Do you think I've shock-valued this?—
    Well, just consider
        This humble, red-letter fact:
    Breonna Taylor
        Was slaughtered, in bed, March 13th,
    And her cop killers
        Not fired till June the 23rd.

No charges brought yet –
Justice turns a blind eye to them. [26]

LV.

How does cultural erasure work
Applied against minority involvement
In creating what the dominant, oppressive
Society co-ops and does with what it likes?

White-washing does the trick,
And a nasty trick it is too;
LGBT History removed daily by
Thug-minded bigots on Wikipedia –
'Cause, if you don't already know it,
Nothing can be Gay on that platform.

And in San Francisco, bastion of progress?
Here the city's public works department
Have taken "White"-washing to literal new heights,
Covering Pride and racial Community murals
Beneath the homogeny of 'anti-vandal' cream paint.

It was entirely bad enough when
The fifty-heart mural in this city for the Pulse victims
Had its Pulse dedication painted over –
Making this powerful LGBT memorial merely
"Pretty," like a fucking 'left my heart' in SF
Piece of meaningless, tourist bullshit.

But now, the just-complete entire wall of a building
Praising Gay unity, covered over during the night.
While a little while before, another mural –
A portrait of multiracial unity – was
Covered over by Public Works.

Public works? A branch of city government
Taking it upon themselves to destroy public art
Erected on private property by the land's owners?

Something's rotten in the state of San Francisco –
Some extremist boldly decides from within the agency
Which minority art will get white-powered and erased. [27]

LVI.
> *"If you're privileged, and you know it,*
> *Raise your hand! (Face-Slap)*
> *If you're privileged, and you know it,*
> *Raise your hand! (Face-Slap)*
> *If you're privileged, and you know it,*
> *And you really shit to show it,*
> *If you're privileged, and you know it,*
> *Raise your hand! (Face-Slap)"*

'Reverend' Louis Giglio said, June 14th,
Hunkered down all nice and cozy
On a soundstage with queer-hating CEO
Of Chick-fil-A (hole), and a silent Lecrae,
Evangelized how slavery must be embraced
By every "guilty" caucasian heart as
God's warmest gift to white Privilege.

> *"If you're full of blessèd bull crap,*
> *Shout Hooray! (All-Day)*
> *If you're full of blessèd bull crap,*
> *Shout Hooray! (All-Day)*
> *If you're full of blessèd bull crap,*
> *Saying "I'm saved" like a dumb sap*
> *If you're full of blessèd bull crap,*
> *Shout Hooray! (All-Day)"*

The *thing* that built this country
And white empires throughout the world
As *His* wish – yeah, go on and say it –
As God's "white blessing." How can
This shit be made up – how dark can

The ultra-satanic heart of the white-devil
Really, possibly be . . . ? How could
Anyone feel comfortable saying this – ever –
Never mind in front of a Black Community
Representative. W. T. F.

> *"If you're god-afeared and own it,*
>   *Pass the ammo! (Amen-O)*
> *If you're god-afeared and own it,*
>   *Pass the ammo! (Amen-O)*
> *If you're god-afeared and own it,*
>   *then your gun will surely show it.*
> *If you're god-afeared and you own it,*
>   *Pass the ammo! (Amen-O)"* [28]

LVII.

"I can't wait"

The summer's heat is about to burst
Like a stifling bubble atop of us.
But here's a question to ask of our times:
Will these tensions soon seem quaint . . . ?

> Three North Carolina policemen were
> Terminated on June the 25th.
> They'd been recorded 20 days before,
> And here are some things they actually said:
> Their police department's only concern
> Was "kneeling down with the black folks," and
> One particular Black officer was
> "bad news." Then adding, "Let's see how his boys
> Take care of him when shit gets rough. See if
> They don't put a bullet in his head."
> Their next topic was a Black woman who'd
> Been detained the day before, calling her

The "n_gr_" – who should have had "a bullet
In her head right then, and move on," they said.
Next, an African American judge
Got called that "fucking n_gr_ magistrate,"
Before moving on to their *coup de grace.*
These men in uniform, so-called servants
To the ideals of 'To Serve and Protect',
Talked of buying the newest assault rifles
For the racial civil war they've dreamed of.
Soon "We are just going to go out and
Start slaughtering them F_____ N_____!"
"I can't wait," was said then. "God; I can't wait."
"Wipe 'em off the fucking map. That'll put
Them back about four or five generations."

So, summer's worst heat is about to burst,
And unless the good people can stop it now,
Next 4th of July might be a bloodbath,
While we're swept along in a war
The Helter Skelter extremists dreamt of. [29]

LVIII.

per aequoreas rauco imitatio
Decimus Junius Juvenalis

A TOAST!

Join me in raising a big glass
Of semi-sweet rosé
For the Karens of the Moment.

A TOAST!

To privileged hordes of princesses
Just getting in the way
And "speakin' to the manager."

Raise a glass to all the hissy-fitters,
Slamming groceries on supermarket floors
As a *serves-you-right* to clerks requesting
That they wear a mask in the checkout line.

One for all the sally-forthers who block
Cars in parking lots with their big asses,
Then waltz up to the police they have called
On Black families just doing some shopping;
Or that blond princess blocking a guy's way
For daring to enter his own apartment building.
Nat'rally for her, breathing-while-Black is enough
To detain him at their front door with a
'Papers, please,' 'I don't believe you' mindset,
And then sally-forthing in front of him,
Onto the elevator, to cover buttons,
Finally stalking him all the way to his front door.
Worst part: she'd do it all over again.

Let's raise a Kosher glass to the woman
At a Target Starbucks who demanded
A server remove her 'BLM' mask
Just because she found it "so offensive,"
Before so offensively dragging in
The Holocaust to serve her princess ways;
One'd think solidarity among all
Minorities would be a given, but –
Not for the self-entitled Karens of today.

Here's a cheer for cop-call Karens:
The 911-dialer on a birdwatcher
In New York's Central Park; her hateful words,
"He's threatening my life," for asking her
To leash her dog in the park's bird preserve.
One for San Francisco's infamous Narc,
Calling the fuzz on a chalk-stenciling guy

Placing Black Lives Matter on his own curb,
But Princess Karen 'KNOWING' the 'owner'
And it wasn't a Queer Latin guy like him –
Except, it was. Gay families still not wanted
In *her* Pacific Heights neighborhood.

And dare we leave out the spittoon-Karens?
Oh, no – for they've earned a special salaam
Like the woman who coughed on a young mom
Acting all *uppity,* asking Karen
To mask up and protect her young children;
Or the *lawyer* who went the extra mile and
Felt fully entitled amongst activists to
Hock a loogie and spit it in a kid's face.

SO TOAST!

Raise your clenched pinot grigio
To the privileged Karens
Whose rights to *protest* won't be quashed.

A TOAST!

To the sobering fact our nation,
Strug'ling in times of woe,
Has lost its collective damn mind. [30]

LIX.
Rage, Rage, Rage –
   our country's lost,
      set adrift
         on an ocean
           of Rage.

LX.

Amongst all the horror,
   One statistic, one statistic among many,
   Says so much.

   On the day George Floyd had his life
   Slowly squeezed out of him,

   Five others were shot and killed by police,
   On the very. Same. Day.

   And guess what? The day those six died
   Was a quiet cop-killing day
   In America. [31]

LXI.

Say Their Names II

Harum-Scarum backlash . . .

   The powers that be
   Lash out in ways reckless,
   Irresponsibly set
   To demonstrate to us
   Who remains in control.
   Just think how Colinford Mattis
   And Urooj Rahman have fared,
   Falsely arrested in Brooklyn
   For 'disrespecting' a cop car
   Already burned out by others,

These two privileged-but-Black lawyers
Were hauled in like common vandals.
After completing bail hearings
For the hyped-up, unprovable
Vandalism charges, they were
Released on bond amounts fitting
To such inconsequential 'crime.'
Then, after being home, a "judge" –
So-called, 'cause a Trump appointee –
Had them arrested *again,* and
Held over for trial without bail.
Say their names: Colinford Mattis
And Urooj Rahman still rotting
In a New York city jail today.

Harum-Scarum backlash . . .

Say the name of Terron J. Boone,
Cop-killed less than two weeks after
His brother Robert Fuller was
Hanged on a tree outside L.A. –
Coincidence L.A. sheriffs
Would just happen to go looking
For a lynching victim's family
To make further "example" of?
Of course, conveniently for them,
Their body cameras were turned off,
So it's their word of what happened
Against that of a dead man. Nice.

Harum-Scarum backlash . . .

Or Helter Skelter scheme –
Have boogie-woogie days

And cop nights of "slaughter"
Been happening all along,
To prove who's in control? [32]

¤{ }¤{ }¤{ }¤{ }¤
¤{ }¤{ }¤{ }¤
¤{ }¤{ }¤
¤{ }¤

Part Nine: Can Kicked Down the Road

But Where Will We Live . . . III

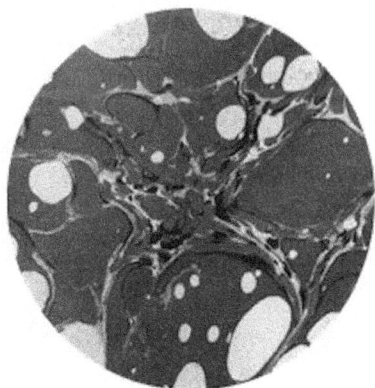

LXII.

Words are my emotional
Stock in trade –

Sometimes I wish
I were out of business.

LXIII.

Each year climate change modelers
At universities around the world
Update their software with data
Collected as actual happenings
On the globe the previous year.
Spring 2020, when this was all done,
Emails flew between the experts:
"Did you get the same results?" they all asked.
For based on last year's trending facts,
All the world's supercomputers confirmed
The climate was in its death throes.
But instead of embracing these hard facts,
These experts looked for ways to break
The accuracy of their own programs.
Faith had interfered with the ones
The public has need to most rely on
For sourcing empiric science –
Not ones to wring hands and say "This must be wrong,"
Just because they don't want to 'believe'
The horror of the findings in black and white –
When they should have been warning us
The seesaw tipping-point is past going back.
How did even our researchers
get to such corrupt, ostrich-in-the-sand
convolutions meant to do harm?

Like all things we do, following the money,
If we dare; climate modeling
Succumbs to faith-based degeneracy,
For as the old, dirt-common prayer
Lays out in bareness: "There's no health in us." [33]

LXIV.

What wells up beneath the human
Cesspit of destructive instinct
To piss our graffiti mark
On accomplishments and "punish"
Nature for making us so truly inconsequential.

> Two-thousand-year-old Joshua Trees
>   Pushed over and killed in the Gop
>   Joke of a government shutdown, laying off
>   National Park Rangers all across the land.

> Covid lockdown serves as an excuse for
>   White 'hunters' on vacay in Africa to
>   Murder a silverback gorilla in June, 2020,
>   While how many rhinos and elephants
>   must die too? The answer, all of them.

> Uncontrolled wildfires in Australia at the end of 2019
>   Were allowed to bring koalas to the point of
>   extinction in the wild, thanks to years of encroachment
>   and rampant bush fires. There's our mark on Australia.

> And what's to be next? Maybe pandas will go
>   Extinct this fire season-or-next in China, if all
>   The poachers don't get to them first while the
>   Government is looking away, dealing with the next virus.

What wells up beneath the human
Cesspit of destructive instinct
To piss our graffiti mark
On accomplishments and "punish"
Nature for making us so truly inconsequential. [34]

LXV.

Summer 2020 is a special time.
A re-set moment button pushed
To teeter humanity on an edge.
Tip one way, it's back to 'normal'
And the certain times of hell to follow;
Tip it back the way of correction –
Of reflection; of positive action
As opposed to passive hand-wringing –
And maybe, we'll have a chance.
    maybe

LXVI.

   von . . . in Todesbanden

Den Tod niemand zwingen kunnt
Bei allen Menschenkindern,
Das macht' alles unsre Sünd,
Kein Unschuld war zu finden.
Davon kam der Tod so bald
Und nahm über uns Gewalt,
Hielt uns in seinem Reich gefangen.
  Halleluja.
                    —Martin Luther

from . . . in Contract with Death

Not one of us can Death command,
Nor the combined might of our kids,
For trying feeds the root of sin,
Sapping the health from the rest of us.
Death wars and loots from us early
By the caprice of his command
Steals us away as captives for his domain. [35]
   Alleluia.

                             —Martin Luther

¤{ }¤{ }¤{ }¤{ }¤
¤{ }¤{ }¤{ }¤
¤{ }¤{ }¤
¤{ }¤

Part Ten: Handbasket
Finale, True Colors

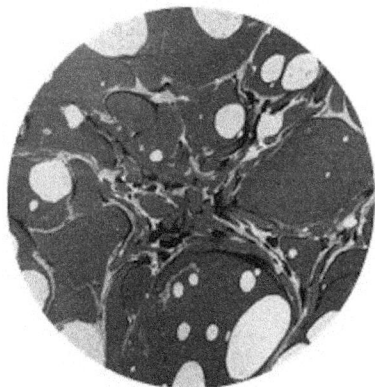

LXVII.

"For even now, the ax has been laid bare
Before the root of the trees, so that
Each failing to bring forth an honest harvest
Might be taken down and fed to the flames."
—Book of Matthew 3:10

LXVIII.

Our checkout baskets ever fuller groan
    For what items we think we've packed away
    The cost racks the sum we'll have to pay
To unpack one by one as a hot stone.
With no means to avoid now, or postpone,
    The Reckoning's total stands in our way
    Before we move another foot today
And vast is our bill to the final Unknown.
        The environment falls about our ears,
        While plagues pandemic – political and
        Blood-red sick like coronavirus tears –
        Fell every human hope bludgeoned by fears
        From a Police State's bigoted command,
        Spelling doom on our fast-come End-of-Years.

LXIX.

i.
Shells

    Across German forests the fires now rage
        As they do all around the globe,
    But among the hard-wood roots are bombs
        Sown in war, the blind xenophobe,

To kill, to maim, to hurt those yet unborn,
    To lay in wait for the right time,
Wreaking paused revenge on the innocent,
    And make son pay for father-crime.

As metaphor, the fact is very apt,
    For much of what's buried today
Will naturally not have impact until
    Future first-responders must stray
Upon the malice we've let go to seed
    And explode on the innocent
Who'll have to deal with the mess we're making
    And bury more dead in lament.

ii.
Economic Rain Forests

Biodiversity's concept model
    Speaks to more than ecology,
For as forests need plants both large and small,
    Small business now dies in a spree
From government interfering, cyber
    Spying from abroad, and Covid –
Four horsemen poised to shutter every door
    And take neighborhoods off the grid.

Let the small plants die, and nothing survives –
    This emergency is poised, rife
To extinguish the economy as
    We've known it in modern life.
Let the economic undergrowth fade
    And trunks of billion-dollar firms
Will be starved of all they need to make jobs
    And will topple, fodder for worms.

iii.
Virulent Buffoons
Swinging in the Treetops

The political plague we've suffered through
    Can be traced back to a "Bonzo"
Sent to Washington on a tide of lies –
    A coot called Reagan, and new low –
One now revealed on tape to have referred
    To Black diplomats as "monkeys";
In the White House, *in* the Oval Office,
    Getting "Yeah"s from Gop flunkies.

From that horrible 'man' with no ideals
    We've been on a soapbox derby
Heading downhill at breakneck speed, till now
    We see, the road to Hell's swervy
With every possible sin, even treason
    Enough to scare Benedict Arnold
From ever having a bad thought again,
    Lest *his* name be slurred with this Donald.

iv.
"Please forgive me"

And so our powder-keg moment ignites
    With the clueless panicked, afraid
Once Humpty Dumpty's shell is cracked open
    All their privileges will be unmade
Exclusive, designed to shield powers that be,
    But for all that's gone and to come,
If we hold one spark to guide us through the night
    It is we're greater than our sum.

America *is* hope, and one man showed
    Us what great power can discern –
Appearing at a BLM protest,
    Holding an honest sign of tact;
"I'm sorry I'm late. I had a lot to learn."
    Hope, contrition, both are needed
As we look around, try to start healing,
    And see where Good has been seeded. [36]

¤{ }¤{ }¤{ }¤{ }¤
¤{ }¤{ }¤{ }¤
¤{ }¤{ }¤
¤{ }¤

Notes and Sources

The updatable nature of the internet means some material documented here may have been moved or deleted. If so, copy the name of the content and content-creator and search online. Alternates will most likely be very easy to find.

ACB

[1] Note for Verse No. 6 (VI):
"They'd ruin all with egotism bidden"

No one has ever liked them for their self-centered ways; not their parents, not their kids, nor their grandkids either. I personally think of them as the "Sell-Out" generation. See Timothy Bracy's undated book review of *A Generation of Sociopaths: How the Baby Boomers Betrayed America*, posted on mensjournal.com

https://www.mensjournal.com/entertain ment/the-age-of-entitlement-how-the-baby-boomers-ruined-everything-w472897/

[2] Note for Verse No. 8 (VIII):
"Trump's S.S. Code"

Make no mistake, Mr. Orange-Glo and his handlers make no mistakes when it comes to neo-nazi white supremacy. See the Jerusalem Post's June 14th, 2020, article *Trump refers to Secret Service as 'S.S.' on Twitter,* posted on jpost.com

https://www.jpost.com/international/trum
p-thanks-ss-for-riot-security-631138

[3] Notes for Verse Nos. 9 & 10 (IX & X):
"Will it ever stop?" and "All the others"
Sadly, the history of the victims listed in these poems are all too easily verifiable through a simple internet search of their names

[4] Note for Verse No. 11 (XI):
"Protest"

The headline. See Adam Gabbatt's June 6th, 2020, article *Protests About Police Brutality Are Met with Wave of Police Brutality Across US,* posted on theguardian.com

https://www.theguardian.com/us-news/2020/jun/06/police-violence-protests-us-george-floyd

[5] Notes for Verse No. 13 (XIII): "OLE HATRED'S SONG"

On workplace protections for members of the Queer minority, Paul said: "[T]he things *you do* in your house, we can just leave those in the house, and they wouldn't have to be part of the workplace[.]" In case that was not clear enough of his contempt for LGBT people, he dug deeper into his personal hell-pit of backwardness with, "[I'll never use] the word 'gay rights,' because I don't really believe in rights based on *your behavior."* [Italics added by me for emphasis]. See the so-called Senator's own words in BallotPedia's article *Rand Paul presidential campaign, 2016/Gay rights*

https://ballotpedia.org/Rand_Paul_presi
dential_campaign,_2016/Gay_rights

– Also see Dominic Holden's March 31st, 2015, article
*Rand Paul Said He Doesn't Believe In The Concept Of
Gay Rights,* posted on buzzfeednews.com

https://www.buzzfeednews.com/article/d
ominicholden/rand-paul-doesnt-believe-
in-the-concept-of-gay-rights

For Rand Paul's almost unbelievable Pro-Lynching stance
(but then again, with the Gops, it's displays of honorable
conduct that would be the real shocker), see the Cable-
Satellite Public Affairs Network's June 4th, 2020, archive
feature *Senator Rand Paul Blocks Emmett Till Anti-Lynching
Bill,* posted on c-span.org

https://www.c-span.org/video/?c4879673/senator-rand-paul-blocks-emmett-till-anti-lynching-bill

For the pair of Black men found hanged on trees in front of important civic structures, see Andrew Blankstein and Phil Helsel's June 15th, 2020, article *Feds to Review Investigations Into Two Black Men Found Hanging in Southern California,* posted on nbcnews.com

https://www.nbcnews.com/news/us-news/feds-review-investigations-two-black-men-found-hanging-southern-california-n1231139

If any part of you still thinks this could be 'fake news,' read the testimony of a North Carolina lawyer who barely escaped a broad daylight lynching attempt on the July 4th holiday in his hometown. See the transcript of Amy Goodman's July 13th, 2020, interview *Attempted Lynching in Indiana. No Arrests? Meet the Survivor: Human Rights Commissioner Vauhxx Booker,* posted on democracynow.org

https://www.democracynow.org/2020/7/
13/vauhxx_booker_attempted_lynching_
indiana

[6] Note for Verse No. 15 (XV):
"How long the day of reckoning"

Dust bowl conditions may convert the central regions of
North America into deserts. See Fiona Harvey's May 18th,
2020, article *Dust Bowl Conditions of 1930s US Now More
Than Twice as Likely to Reoccur*, posted on
theguardian.com

https://www.theguardian.com/environme
nt/2020/may/18/us-dust-bowl-
conditions-likely-to-reoccur-great-plains

[7] Notes for Verse No. 17 (XVII):
"Good News!"

Some things are much too awful to make credible fiction. For reactivated giant viruses, see Stefan Sirucek's March 3rd, 2014, article *Ancient "Giant Virus" Revived from Siberian Permafrost – Climate Change Could Release More,* posted on nationalgeographic.com

https://www.nationalgeographic.com/news/2014/3/140303-giant-virus-permafrost-siberia-pithovirus-pandoravirus-science/

For the tons of microplastic already pouring down on our heads, see Matt Simon's June 11th, 2020, article *Plastic Rain is the New Acid Rain,* posted on wired.com

https://www.hcn.org/articles/climate-
desk-pollution-the-wests-invisible-
menace-microplastics

For the gross disregard of States' rights to determine local policy (in this case, so lil Dumpy Jr. can "hunt" anything he fancies), see Darryl Fears' June 9th, 2020, article *Trump Administration Makes It Easier for Hunters to Kill Bear Cubs and Wolf Pups in Alaska,* posted on washingtonpost.com

https://www.washingtonpost.com/climate-
environment/2020/06/08/trump-administration-
make-it-easier-hunters-kill-alaska-bear-cubs-
wolf-pups/

For the conservation officer (!) ordered to kill orphaned bear cubs, see Leyland Cecco's June 11th, 2020, article *Canadian Conservation Officer Fired for Refusing to Kill Bear Cubs Wins Legal Battle*, posted on Washington post.com

https://www.theguardian.com/world/202
0/jun/11/bryce-casavant-canada-
conservation-officer-bear-cubs-legal-
battle

[8] Notes for Verse No. 18 (XVIII):
"HYMN"

As already mentioned in the note to Verse No. 15, there's published analysis the central part of the United States is now primed, through excessive droughts and ever-rising temperatures, for permanent dust-bowl conditions to settle over the region. The *good news* is, the locust swarms are already here to stay. See Gro Intelligence's June 18th, 2020, article *Locust Swarm Could Threaten India's Next Crop,* posted on gro-intelligence.com

https://gro-
intelligence.com/insights/articles/locust-
swarm-could-threaten-india-s-next-crop

Time to pay the reaper on the climate emergency. See
Justin Worland's July 9th, 2020, article *2020 Is Our Last,
Best Chance to Save the Planet,* posted on time.com

https://time.com/5864692/climate-
change-defining-moment/

[9] Notes for Verse No. 23 (XXIII):
"Dog-whistle politics eat their brains"

As a doddering old man, no one other than North Korean
dictator Kim has hit the nail so squarely on the head (or,
hairplugs – whichever the case may be). See Randy
Rainbow's September 25th, 2017, video *How Do You Solve
a Problem Like Korea?,* posted on youtube.com

https://youtu.be/580dYcYCneA

Trump's outright seditious call to overturn the Constitution, via the means of a racially fueled civil war, is not as secretive to reasonable people as he thinks ('think' applied loosely in his case, of course…). See Jeff Sharlet's June 22nd, 2020, article *"You Know What to Do": Decoding the Grotesque Symbolism of Trump's Tulsa Rally,* posted on theatlantic.com

https://www.vanityfair.com/news/2020/0 6/decoding-the-grotesque-symbolism-of- trumps-tulsa-rally

[10] Note for Verse No. 24 (XXIV):
"In the ign'rant psychosis of the times"

Trump's schoolyard level or accusing others of what he knows to be heinous crimes in himself is a mental illness technically known as "Projection." See James Fallows' October 16th, 2016, article *Why Does Trump 'Project' So Much? A Hypotheses,* posted on theatlantic.com

https://www.theatlantic.com/notes/2016/
10/why-does-trump-project-so-much-a-
hypothesis/504293/

[11] Notes for Verse No. 28 (XXVIII):
"Minstrel Faces, 2020"

The use of peaceful protesters blocking major traffic arteries was invented by ACT UP in the mid-1980s. All protests organized around this concept knowingly or unknowingly owe a debt of respect to Larry Kramer and his HIV/AIDS activism. For the origins of *Silence = Death,* see the Brooklyn Museum's 1987 example of one of the group's original protest banner, posted on brooklynmuseum.org

https://www.brooklynmuseum.org/openc
ollection/objects/159258

For a Stepin Fetchit moment, see Harlem Renaissance
TIME TRAVEL Radio Show's March 28th, 2017, posting
Stepin Fetchit Excerpt from 'Judge Priest' 1934, posted on
youtube.com

https://youtu.be/kvaD2HbI3dk

For the 2017 BLM banning of Gay cops and their family from
their own Community Pride events, see Rinaldo Walcott's
June 28th, 2017, article *Black Lives Matter, police and Pride,*
posted on the conversation.com

https://theconversation.com/black-lives-
matter-police-and-pride-toronto-
activists-spark-a-movement-79089

[12] Note for Verse No. 29 (XXIX):
"DEFINITION"

Cops gloating over their murder victims as they lie dying. That their killings have been so brutal, a public viewing of the remains will not be performed seems to be another of those Depraved Heart 101 lessons from the police academies. I know I have read about these exact remarks having been said by officers several times. For its use against Sean Reed, unarmed and shot 13 times, see Britni de la Cretaz's May 7th, 2020, article *Why the Killings of Sean Reed and Ahmaud Arbery Are Being Called Lynchings,* posted on refinery29.com

https://www.refinery29.com/en-us/2020/05/9789855/sean-reed-ahmaud-arbery-video-black-death-lynching

[13] Notes for Verse No. 31 (XXXI):
"All in good fun – what bullshit"

Twisted minstrel portrayals of minority groups wear many shades of shoe polish. For Dana Carvey's "Chickenman" Asian blackface, see the June 1st, 2017, article *'SNL' Skit Demonstrates Lack of Representation,* posted on rafu.com

https://www.rafu.com/2017/06/snl-skit-demonstrates-lack-of-representation/

For Alexandrea Borstein's "Ms. Swan" Asian blackface, see batmanproductions' *Miss Swan Dating Game,* posted on youtube.com

https://youtu.be/I6ptoDmvCKI

For Jimmy Fallons' "Scrooge" Gay blackface, see Saturday Night Live's December 22, 2013, *Christmas Past – SNL,* posted on youtube.com

https://www.youtube.com/watch?v=Lb36
BwPa7pQ

For a sample of Fred Arminsen's endless supply of homophobic Gay blackface, see Praneeth Karkera's October 21st, 2011, *Excuse Me – Eurotrip,* posted on youtube.com

https://www.youtube.com/watch?v=_Mr
BpmM5YAM

For the TV show Modern Family's Gay-as-pedophile blackface, see Ole Markus moen's April 21st, 2016, *Modern Family – Best Moments S0501,* posted on youtube.com

https://youtu.be/1INif-coH8I

[14] Note for Verse No. 32 (XXXII):
"And...What About Equal Justice"

Once it was a potentially benign symbol, but quickly grew to be the freak flag of white supremacy in the nation's militarized cop forces. See Maurice Chammah and Cary Aspinwall's June 8th, 2020, article *The Short, Fraught History of the 'Thin Blue Line' American Flag,* posted on themarshallproject.org

https://www.themarshallproject.org/2020/06/08/
the-short-fraught-history-of-the-thin-blue-line-
american-flag

[15] Note for Verse No. 33 (XXXIII):
"From east to west come desert sand"

The effects of the climate emergency spread in all directions. See Evan Gough's July 14th, 2020, article *Incredible Sahara Dust Plume Sweeping Across the Atlantic is Largest on Record,* posted on sciencealert.com

https://www.sciencealert.com/watch-this-incredible-plume-of-dust-from-africa-cross-the-entire-atlantic-ocean

[16] Note for Verse No. 36 (XXXVI):
"Worse yet, I can't afford water"

The cost of drinking water has exploded in the US, despite the fact that working-class people cannot rely on it to drink anymore, thanks to Gop politicizing of the EPA's reason for being. See Nina Lakhani's June 23rd, 2020, article *Revealed: Millions of Americans Can't Afford Water as Bills Rise 80% in a Decade,* posted on theguardian.com

https://www.theguardian.com/us-news/2020/jun/23/millions-of-americans-cant-afford-water-bills-rise

[17] Notes for Verse No. 38 (XXXVIII):
"From Flint, Michigan, to Russian arctic oil spill"

The environmental effect of the massive Russian arctic oil spill is still years away from understanding. The one thing that's certain is the contamination occurred because of global melting of permafrost, so we can expect these spills to be ongoing events from now on. See Brendan Cole's June 30th, 2020, article *Firm in Russian Arctic Oil Spill Probe Admits Pumping Waste into Tundra,* posted on newsweek.com

https://www.newsweek.com/russia-nornickel-arctic-pollution-greenpeace-1514300

If you go to Google News and search for "tap water flames," several dozen stories, all of less than a month's age, will show you just how corporate-contaminated American drinking water is. See Susan Phillips' June 15th, 2020, article *Pennsylvania Attorney General Charges Cabot Oil and Gas with Environmental Crimes,* posted on whyy.org

https://whyy.org/articles/pa-attorney-general-charges-cabot-oil-and-gas-with-environmental-crimes/

– Also see this all-too sadly iconic expose: Chris Matyszczyk's January 2nd, 2014, article *Man Sets Tap Water on Fire, Sparks Debate,* posted on cnet.com

https://www.cnet.com/news/man-sets-tap-water-on-fire-sparks-debate/

[18] Notes for Verse No. 39 (XXXIX):
"Is it any wonder Pollyanna journalistic"

There has already been up to an 80% die-off of the planet's insect populations. See Damian Carrington's February 12th, 2020, article *Car 'Splatometer' Tests Reveal Huge Decline in Number of Insects,* posted on theguardian.com

https://www.theguardian.com/environme
nt/2020/feb/12/car-splatometer-tests-
reveal-huge-decline-number-insects

Gop interference in government attempts to understand the causes of Gulf War Syndrome, to treat "Our Troops," was shamefully exposed (and ignored) in the Clinton Administration. See David Olinger's January 11th, 1997, article *Researcher Says Work's Tie to War Illness Got Him Fired,* posted on getipm.com

http://www.getipm.com/government/mos
s.htm

[19] Note for Verse No. 41 (XLI):
"I sigh and wonder why"

Unless you think of month-on-month record-shattering high temperature and air pollution a good thing, then we've wasted all the time we had to stabilize the Earth for continued human habitation. See Stephanie Ebbs' *(et al)* July 3rd, 2020, article *Temperatures and Carbon Dioxide Are Up, Regulations Are Down: May Set a Record for Above-Average Temperatures and CO2 is at an All-Time High*, posted on abcnews.go.com

https://abcnews.go.com/Politics/tempera
tures-carbon-dioxide-regulations-
environmental-headlines-missed-
week/story?id=71583312

[20] Note for Verse No. 42 (XLII):
"Those Sitting on Thorns"

The wide-spread encroachment on people's Constitutional Rights has been accelerating since the Bush Jr. Administration. Has it all been done in the name of the obscene "industry" of outsourced, for-profit prison corporations, which the Gops legalized under the reign of that toad, Gingrich? See Stephen Carter's December 4th, 2014, article *With So Many Laws, We Could All Be Felons*, posted on chicagotribune.com

https://www.chicagotribune.com/opinion/
commentary/ct-eric-garner-laws-felons-
chokehold-perspec-1125-20141204-
story.html

[21] Note for Verse No. 45 (XLV):
"June Rollcall at the Supreme Court"

The Supreme Court knows it's pushed the Gop agenda too dangerously far already, and societal pressure this summer has forced a retreat of the justices to more Constitutional stands. See the David G. Savage's June 24th, 2020, article *Major Rulings from Supreme Court in 2020 Term on Abortion, Religion and Trump Taxes*, posted on latimes.com

https://www.latimes.com/politics/story/20
20-06-24/supreme-court-2020-term-
major-cases

[22] Notes for Verse No. 47 (XLVII):
"This election year, I stumbled upon"

Recordings of the election speeches of 1912 show just how backwards this country has been driven by Gop politicking in recent times. For the Democratic candidate, see ForgottenHistoryUSA's January 18th, 2009, posting *1912 US Election Campaign Speech Audio – Woodrow Wilson,* posted on youtube.com

https://youtu.be/-PI9QimYXSQ

For the Progressive candidate, see ForgottenHistoryUSA's January 19th, 2009, posting *1912 US Election Campaign Speech Audio – Theodore Roosevelt,* posted on youtube.com

https://youtu.be/lxi3fwGvLsw

For the Republican candidate, see SlickRickNixon's July 18th, 2015, posting *William H. Taft "Who Are the People?" Speech (1912),* posted on youtube.com

https://youtu.be/OkqEm85ou-8

[23] Notes for Verse No. 48 (XLVIII):
"Divide & Conquer"

The debauched snicker of lil Bushy Jr. should have kept him out of the presidential race to begin with. See the David Letterman Show's November 13th, 2006, brief rundown *George W Bush – Inexplicable Laugh,* posted on youtube.com

https://youtu.be/HlFqFFoaoe8

Compare Jr.'s devious sniggering tendencies with a puerile cartoon show's character named "Butthead". This show premiered long before the Supreme Court appointed Cheney-Bush as 'president' of the U.S.

https://youtu.be/A6j4ZClZlyY

As for the stakes being too high for foreign powers to allow tired old Dump to be taken out with the White House garbage in November, Kremlin hackers only have to raise the shadow of a doubt about the returns for one of two "toss up" states to usher in a nightmare scenario on how the two-time national election loser will stay in power for his Russian owners. See the method in Deborah Golden Alecson's July 12, 2020, article

Cowering Under the Covers: Is it Really Possible for a Democrat to win in 2020 with the Russians Proceeding Full Speed Ahead to Intervene on Trump's Behalf?, posted on theberkshireedge.com

https://theberkshireedge.com/cowering-under-the-covers-2/

[24] Note for Verse No. 49 (XIL):
"The Heavy Toll of 'Leadership'"

This poem relies on information contained in Alex Nichols' August 14th, 2017, article *Political Correctness Doesn't Kill People,* posted on theoutline.com

https://theoutline.com/post/2102/political-correctness-doesn-t-kill-people?zd=1&zi=ibyrmzlc

[25] Note for Verse No. 53 (LIII):
"This summer, Death unchecked across the land"

Madman insists the American public be made uninsured during the worst global epidemic in 100 years. See Sahil Kapur's June 25th, 2020, article *Trump administration asks Supreme Court to strike down Obamacare amid pandemic; recession,* posted on nbcnews.com

https://www.nbcnews.com/politics/donal d-trump/trump-administration-asks-supreme-court-strike-down-obamacare-amid-pandemic-n1232203

[26] Note for Verse No. 54 (LIV):
"Meanwhile, back in Louisville"

As of this day of writing, July 13th, 2020, no accounting for the actions of Breonna Taylor's murders are underway. None. Hear National Public Radio's broadcast from 5:08 AM this morning, entitled *No Arrests or Charges so far in the Breonna Taylor Shooting Death,* posted on npr.org

https://www.npr.org/2020/07/13/890328
388/no-arrests-or-charges-so-far-in-
breonna-taylors-shooting-death

[27] Notes for Verse No. 55 (LV):
"How does cultural erasure work"

LGTB Pride mural is covered over by San Francisco Public
Works Department. See Amanda Bartlett's June 25th, 2020,
article *'We will not be erased': Graffiti Artist Strikes Back
After SF Queer Bar's Mural is Painted Over During Pride,*
posted on sfgate.com

https://www.sfgate.com/sf-
culture/slideshow/The-mural-on-SF-s-
oldest-queer-bar-was-painted-
204388.php

Racial Unity mural is covered over by San Francisco Public Works Department. See Teresa Hammerl's June 8th, 2020, article *Public Works Paints Over Kantine's 'Unity & Connection' Mural Just Hours After Installation,* posted on hoodline.com

https://hoodline.com/2020/06/public-works-paints-over-kantine-s-unity-connection-mural-just-hours-after-installation

[28] Note for Verse No. 56 (LVI):
"If you're privileged, and you know it"

Louie Giglio is a 'Reverend' who deserves zero reverence. See Minyvonne Burke's June 17th, 2020, article *Atlanta Pastor Who Suggested Slavery Was a 'Blessing' to White People Apologizes,* posted on nbcnews.com

https://www.nbcnews.com/news/us-news/atlanta-pastor-who-suggested-slavery-was-blessing-white-people-apologizes-n1231325?cid=referral_taboolafeed

– Also see the original video of the 'Rev's white-power comments.*

https://youtu.be/X14_5PJMeos

*Now we know what farting dog-whistle comes out of their mouth each time they say "Bless you"

[29] Note for Verse No. 57 (LVII):
"I can't wait"

This poem relies on information contained in Khaleda Rahman's June 25th, 2020, article *Police Officer Fired for Saying He Can't Wait to Slaughter Black People,* posted on newsweek.com

https://www.newsweek.com/three-officers-fired-racist-comments-1513286

[30] Notes for Verse No. 58 (LVIII):
"A TOAST!" The Latin dedication says *In raucous imitation of Juvenal*

Now, let's step aside and view a few of the many Karens Behaving Badly in action for ourselves

– Groceries Slamming Karen:

https://youtu.be/tZQXoZRO7FM

– Kroger Karen:

https://youtu.be/e3RmTRO6vyE

– Door-Bouncer Karen:

https://youtu.be/3xpjWaR4z3Y

– The So Offensive Karen:

https://youtu.be/jf_ymaT-3OA

– Narc: *noun* (informal) a person who informs on others for actions perceived as transgressive; specifically, to any type of authority figure, such as parents, cops, teachers, bosses, etc.

https://www.urbandictionary.com/define.php?term=narc

– Birdwatcher 911 Karen:

https://youtu.be/iUQWd4q3tjA

– San Francisco Karen:

https://youtu.be/fYJRL9b89ol

– Coughing Karen:

https://youtu.be/Eih90P6WePM

– Spittoon-Karen:

https://youtu.be/Egb7deRss6A

[31] Note for Verse No. 60 (LX):
"One statistic among many"

At least five others were shot and killed by police on the same day George Floyd was asphyxiated. See Melissa Segura's June 27th, 2020, article *On the Day George Died, Police Across the U.S. Shot and Killed at Least Five Other Men,* posted on buzzfeednews.com

https://www.buzzfeednews.com/article/
melissasegura/george-floyd-other-men-
killed-by-police

– Also see the website Mapping Police Violence, which provides statistics and tracks Americans killed by the police:

https://mappingpoliceviolence.org/

[32] Notes for Verse No. 61 (LXI):
"Say Their Names II"

For how Colinford Mattis and Urooj Rahman's legal rights have been shamelessly "Trumped" upon, see Murtaza Hussain's June 19th, 2020, article *Two Brooklyn Lawyers Accused of Throwing Molotov Cocktails Are the Public Face of Trump Administration's Crackdown on Dissent,* posted on theintercept.com

https://theintercept.com/2020/06/19/broo klyn-lawyers-molotov-cocktails-trump/

One of the injured survivors of the police killing of Terron J. Boone gives an account in Matthew Ormseth's June 24, 2020, article *Woman Injured in Shorting of Terron Boone Files Civil Rights Claim,* posted on latimes.com

https://www.latimes.com/california/story/
2020-06-24/woman-injured-during-
terron-boone-shooting-files-civil-rights-
claim

[33] Notes for Verse No. 63 (LXIII):
"Each year climate change modelers"

The doomsday scenarios predicted by every institution in the world generated a "That can't be right" enabler-fest within the supposed scientific community the public relies on for facts and not belief. See Jeff Berardelli's July 1st, 2020, article *Some New Climate Models are Projecting Extreme Warming. Are they Correct?,* posted on yaleclimateconnections.org

https://www.yaleclimateconnections.org/
2020/07/some-new-climate-models-are-
projecting-extreme-warming-are-they-
correct/

For the eroding of science by faith-based bias, see Gonçalo Prista's March 23rd, 2020, article *A Reflection on Current Academia Reality: Is It Gaining Religious Features?,* posted on euroscientist.com

https://www.euroscientist.com/a-reflection-on-current-academia-reality-is-it-gaining-religious-features/

[34] Notes for Verse No. 64 (LXIV):
"What wells up beneath the human"

Scurrilous Gop politicking allows vandals to topple two-thousand-year-old national monuments. See Aria Bendix's February 1st, 2019, article *It Could Take 300 Years for Joshua Tree National Park to Recover from the Government Shutdown,* posted on businessinsider.com

https://www.businessinsider.com/joshua-tree-national-park-damage-government-shutdown-2019-1

Pandemic lockdowns allow for unmonitored 'hunting' of critically endangered species. See Dina Fine Maron's

July 9th, 2020, article *Pandemic-Induced Poaching Surges in Uganda,* posted on nationalgeographic.com

https://www.nationalgeographic.com/animals/2020/07/covid19-behind-uganda-poaching/

Loss of habitat for the koala bear is due to human environmental mismanagement. See Nick Visser's June 30th, 2020, article *Koalas May Go Extinct in the Wild By 2050 in Australia's New South Wales,* posted on huffpost.com

https://www.huffpost.com/entry/koalas-extinct-in-wild-new-south-wales_n_5efad0c7c5b612083c520c74

[35] Notes for Verse No. 66 (LXVI):
"in Todesbanden"

Christ lag in Todesbanden ("Christ Lain in Contract with Death") by Martin Luther, 1524, was set to music by J.S. Bach (BWV 4). The entire libretto can be found on Emmanuel Music's program notes for the 2019/2020 season.

http://www.emmanuelmusic.org/notes_tr
anslations/translations_cantata/t_bwv00
4.htm

– Also see this performance of "Den Tod niemand zwingen kunnt" from 2009 featuring David Pla and Llorenç Niclòs as soloists.

https://youtu.be/iRSdkhQ0e8s

[36] Notes for Verse No. 69 (LXIX):
i. "Shells"

Second World War shells are hampering modern firefighting efforts. See Christopher Woody's August 2nd, 2018, article *Record heat is stoking wildfires in Europe – and it's setting off leftover bombs from World War II,* posted on businessinsider.com

https://www.businessinsider.com/record-heat-in-europe-cause-forest-wildfires-and-explode-world-war-ii-2018-8

ii. "Virulent Buffoons Swinging in the Treetops"

Reagan exposed as real-life Bonzo. See Sarah Mervosh and Niraj Chokshi's July 31st, 2019, article *Reagan Called Africans 'Monkeys' in Call with Nixon, Tape Reveals,* posted on nytimes.com

https://www.nytimes.com/2019/07/31/us/
politics/ronald-reagan-richard-nixon-
racist.html

– Also listen to the recording

https://youtu.be/z7GLJsclRi8

iv. "Please forgive me"

Ryan D. "Wheelz" is the *I'm Sorry I'm Late* hero. See Dan Evon's June 19th, 2020, article *Is This 'I'm Sorry I'm Late. I Had a Lot to Learn' Protest Sign Real?,* posted on snopes.com

https://www.snopes.com/fact-check/im-sorry-im-late-blm-sign/

~

www.ingramcontent.com/pod-product-compliance
Lightning Source LLC
Chambersburg PA
CBHW032003040426
42448CB00006B/468